ENGLISH CONVERSATION
MADE NATURAL

Engaging Dialogues to Learn English

LANGUAGE GURU

TABLE OF CONTENTS

INTRODUCTION

We all know that immersion is the tried and true way to learn a foreign language. After all, it's how we got so good at our first language. The problem is that it's extremely difficult to recreate the same circumstances when we learn a foreign language. We come to rely so much on our native language for everything, and it's hard to make enough time to learn a new one.

We aren't surrounded by the foreign language in our home countries. More often than not, our families can't speak this new language we want to learn. And many of us have stressful jobs or demanding classes that eat away at our limited energy and hours of the day. Immersion can seem like an impossibility.

What we can do, however, is gradually work our way up to immersion no matter where we are in life. And the way we can do this is through extensive reading and listening.

If you have ever taken a foreign language class, chances are you are familiar with the intensive kind of reading and listening. In intensive reading and listening, a small amount of text or a short audio recording is broken down line by line, and then, you are drilled on grammar endlessly.

Extensive reading and listening, on the other hand, is quite the opposite. You read a large number of pages or listen to hours and hours of the foreign language without worrying about understanding everything. You rely on context for meaning and try to limit the number of words you need to look up.

If you ask the most successful language learners, it's not intensive but extensive reading and listening that delivers the best results. Simply, volume is much more effective than explicit explanations and rote memorization.

To be able to read like this comfortably, you must practice reading in the foreign language for hours every single day. It takes a massive volume of text before your brain stops intensively reading and shifts into extensive reading.

This book hopes to provide a few short English-language dialogues that you can use to practice extensive reading. We hope these conversations help build confidence in your overall reading comprehension skills and encourage you to read more native material. They offer supplementary reading practice with a heavy focus on teaching vocabulary words.

Vocabulary is the number one barrier to entry to extensive reading. Without an active vocabulary base of 10,000 words or more, you'll be stuck constantly looking up words in the dictionary, which will be sure to slow down your reading early on. To speed up the rate at which you read, building and maintaining a vast vocabulary range is absolutely vital. This is why it's so important to invest as much time as possible into immersing yourself in native English every single day. This includes both reading and listening as well as being around native speakers through any and all means possible.

We hope you enjoy the book and find it useful in growing your English vocabulary and bringing you a few steps closer to extensive reading and fluency!

HOW TO USE THIS BOOK

To simulate extensive reading better, we recommend keeping things simple and using the dialogues in the following manner. Read through each dialogue just once and no more. In general, whenever you encounter a word you don't know, first try to guess its meaning using the surrounding context. If its meaning is still unclear and the word is <u>underlined</u>, check that chapter's vocabulary list for a very simplified definition. If the unknown word is not underlined, a quick online dictionary search may be required.

In our vocabulary lists, we have strived both to include as many potentially new words and phrases as possible but also to keep each list as brief as possible. As a result, we left out a great deal of words that can be understood via context as well as many basic words.

In addition, it's also recommended to read each dialogue silently. While reading aloud can seem beneficial for pronunciation and intonation, it's a practice more aligned with intensive reading. It will further slow down your reading pace and make it considerably more difficult for you to get into extensive reading. If you want to work on pronunciation and intonation, consider practicing these during study and review times rather than reading time. Alternatively, you could also speak to a English tutor or friend to practice what you learned.

After completing the reading for each chapter, test your knowledge of the dialogue by answering the comprehension questions. Check your answers using the answer key located at the end of the book.

As a means of review, memorization of any kind is completely unnecessary for language acquisition. The actual language acquisition process occurs subconsciously, and any effort to memorize new vocabulary and grammar structures only stores this information in your short-term memory. Attempting to force new information into your long-term memory only serves to eat up your time and make it that much more frustrating when you can't recall it in the future.

If you wish to review new information that you have learned from the dialogues, there are several options that would be wiser. Spaced Repetition Systems (SRS) allow you to cut down on your review time by setting specific intervals in which you are tested on information in order to promote long-term memory storage. Anki and the Goldlist Method are two popular SRS choices that give you the ability to review whatever information you'd like from whatever material you'd like.

Trying to actively review every single new thing you learn, however, will slow you down on your overall path to fluency. While there may be hundreds or even thousands of sentences you want to practice and review, perhaps the best way to go about internalizing it all is to forget it. If it's that important, it will come up through more reading and listening to more English. Languages are more effectively acquired when we allow ourselves to read and listen to them naturally.

And with that, it is time to get started with our main character Charlie and the 30 dialogues from his life. Good luck, reader!

CHAPTER 1:

CHANGING MAJORS

(Charlie has come to the student counseling office to change his major.)

Charlie: I'm just not sure what kind of work i want to do.

Counselor: And that's perfectly normal. A lot of us drift around in life trying to figure out where we belong.

Charlie: Well, it's certainly not chemistry. I can tell you that. I was really good at it in high school, but I just don't think I can do it for the rest of my life.

Counselor: I wish I could tell you what your true passion is. If I could, this whole "choosing a major and career" thing would be much more straightforward now, wouldn't it?

Charlie: You really need a crystal ball at your desk.

Counselor: I know, right? I might as well come to work dressed in a wizard's robe and hat, too.

Charlie: Definitely. For now, I think I'll switch my major to "undecided" and do a little soul searching.

Counselor: That's OK. That's exactly what college is for.

Vocabulary

- <u>counseling</u> --- listening and giving advice to sb. professionally
- <u>major</u> (college) --- the main subject someone studies at college
- <u>perfectly</u> --- completely, in a perfect way
- ✓ <u>drift</u> --- to move slowly without direction
- <u>figure out</u> --- to understand
- <u>belong</u> --- to be in the right place
- <u>chemistry</u> (subject) --- the study of chemicals
- <u>passion</u> --- a very strong feeling of liking or hating something
- <u>whole</u> (important) --- used to show something is important
- <u>straightforward</u> (easy) --- easy to understand
- <u>crystal ball</u> --- a glass ball used by people who say they can see the future
- <u>might as well</u> --- used to suggest sth. when there is nothing better
- <u>wizard</u> (magic) --- a person who can use magic
- <u>robe</u> --- a long loose piece of clothing
- <u>soul searching</u> --- deep thought about your feelings

Comprehension Questions

1. What was Charlie's original major before he decided to switch?
    A. History
    B. Chemistry
    C. Counseling
    D. Wizard

2. What major did Charlie decide to switch to?
    A. Chemistry
    B. Counseling
    C. History
    D. Undecided

3. If someone is doing some "soul searching", what do they really mean?
    A. They lost their soul and are now searching for it.
    B. They are searching for the love of their life.
    C. They are taking time to think over their emotions and motives.
    D. They are hunting ghosts.

CHAPTER 2:
GAMING SESSION

way → adverb.

She finished the race way ahead of the other

→ *I must be going home; it's way past my bedtime*

The price is way above what we can afford

(Charlie goes over to his best friend Ben's house to <u>hang out</u> and play video games.)

very much

Ben: <u>Dang</u> it! I died again. This level is <u>way</u> too hard, <u>man</u>. *going to*

Charlie: Look. We don't have any teamwork. We're never <u>gonna</u> beat this boss by acting separately.

Ben: Our characters are like oil and water. They don't mix together.

Charlie: What if I <u>distract</u> him while you <u>deal</u> as much damage as possible? When he starts <u>targeting</u> you, we will change places.

Ben: So, like a game of <u>cat and mouse</u>?

Charlie: Yeah, but there are two mice. And the mice have <u>weapons</u>.

Ben: Let's try it.

(The two <u>resume</u> playing.)

Ben: Hey, we did it.

Charlie: Yay!

Ben: I can't believe that actually <u>worked</u>. That was great! <u>Yo</u>, we should go out and get a snack to celebrate.

Charlie: Alright. Let's go.

Vocabulary

- <u>session</u> (time) --- a period of time where an activity is done

- <u>hang out</u> --- to spend time at a place or with people

- <u>dang</u> --- a less rude way to say damn

- <u>way</u> [adverb] --- very, very much

- <u>man</u> [exclamation] --- *(slang)* used to show strong feelings

- <u>gonna</u> --- *(informal)* going to

- <u>distract</u> --- to make somebody stop paying attention to sth.

- <u>deal</u> (damage) --- to hit something, to be harmful to something

- <u>target</u> [verb] --- to aim something at something else

- <u>cat and mouse</u> --- a game where someone tries to catch sb.

- <u>weapons</u> --- objects used to fight

- <u>resume</u> --- to continue after stopping

- <u>work</u> (have success) --- to be successful

- <u>yo</u> --- *(slang)* used to greet, to show excitement, or to get sb.'s attention

Comprehension Questions

1. Which two substances do not mix well together?
   A. Oil and water
   B. Salt and water
   C. Sugar and water
   D. Fire and water

2. How do the boys defeat the boss in the game?
   A. They go get snacks to celebrate.
   B. They work together as a team.
   C. They act separately.
   D. They buy better weapons.

3. How do Charlie and Ben celebrate their victory?
   A. They bump their fists.
   B. They play some music.
   C. They go out and get snacks.
   D. They don't celebrate their victory.

CHAPTER 3: CONVENIENCE STORE

(The two are inside their local <u>convenience store</u> <u>browsing</u> the store's <u>shelves</u>.)

Charlie: So, what do you want to eat?
Ben: Let's get sandwiches.

(The boys bring their <u>purchases</u> to the <u>checkout</u> <u>counter</u>. After paying for their food, they go out to eat in Charlie's car.)

Ben: Wow, this is really good. Is that <u>avocado</u> I taste?
Charlie: Avocado and red pepper, I think.
Ben: So, what's <u>going on</u> with you lately? You said that you changed majors.
Charlie: Yeah. I <u>have no idea</u> what I want to do.
Ben: Same. I don't even want to think about it.
Charlie: You <u>eventually</u> have to, right?
Ben: Nope.
Charlie: How about when you <u>turn</u> 30?
Ben: Not then either.
Charlie: 80?
Ben: I will be a <u>gamer</u> to the day I die. You'll be <u>prying</u> the <u>controller</u> out of my cold, dead hands when I'm <u>gone</u>.

Vocabulary

- <u>convenience store</u> --- a small shop that is open late

- <u>browse</u> --- to look around without trying to find anything

- <u>shelves</u> --- flat things on a wall or in a case that you can put stuff on

- <u>purchases</u> --- things you buy

- <u>checkout</u> --- the place in a store where you pay for things

- <u>counter</u> --- a table that is higher and can't be moved

- <u>avocado</u> --- a green and black fruit with a yellow-green inside

- <u>go on</u> (happen) --- to happen

- <u>have no idea</u> --- used to say somebody really doesn't know sth.

- <u>eventually</u> --- in the end

- <u>turn</u> (become) --- to become something, to make sth. become sth.

- <u>gamer</u> --- a person who plays games

- <u>pry</u> (open) --- to use power to separate something from sth. else

- <u>controller</u> (game) --- a tool used to play a game

- <u>gone</u> (not alive) --- dead

-or 打听

She likes to pry into the private life of her friends.

Comprehension Questions

1. In a convenience store, where do you usually pay for your purchases?
    A. At the door
    B. At the office
    C. In the storage room
    D. At the checkout counter

2. Which item are you NOT likely to find in a convenience store?
    A. Sandwiches
    B. Snacks
    C. Drinks
    D. Controllers

3. Where do the boys eat their sandwiches?
    A. Inside the convenience store
    B. Inside Ben's car
    C. Inside Charlie's car
    D. Inside the sandwiches

CHAPTER 4:
ON THE CLOCK

(Charlie works at a local pizza <u>delivery</u> shop as a <u>part-time</u> delivery driver. Inside the store, Charlie and the pizza store's <u>general</u> manager are chatting while <u>folding</u> pizza boxes.)

Lucy: So, I <u>fired</u> him. I understand that things <u>come up</u>, and some days you are going to be late. But a <u>no-call, no-show</u> is <u>inexcusable</u>.

Charlie: I <u>see</u>. He was friendly and fun to be around, but a no-call, no-show is pretty bad.

Lucy: It happens <u>from time to time</u>. So many college kids work here, and some of them want to party all night. Then they are too <u>hungover</u> or tired to come to work. I wish they would just <u>call in</u> at the very least. *or call in sick 請病假*

Charlie: Wow, I think you're the most <u>lenient</u> boss I've ever had.

Lucy: Oh no. I would still fire them if I knew that was the reason they called in. We need a <u>reliable</u> team to <u>run</u> this place.

Charlie: <u>Remind</u> me to never <u>get on your bad side</u>. ✓

Lucy: You'd be one of the first ones I would <u>promote</u>, <u>honestly</u>.

Charlie: Really?

Lucy: A second manager would be nice. I'm here every day, and it's not good for my <u>mental</u> health. I need the <u>time off</u>.

Charlie: Wow. I don't even know what to say.

Lucy: You don't have to. The next order is ready. Go deliver it.

she was very lenient towards him
the judge often passes lenient sentences

Vocabulary

- <u>on the clock</u> (work) --- working right now

- <u>delivery</u> (of things) --- taking things to people

- <u>part-time</u> --- done for only a part of a full work week

- <u>general</u> (lead) --- most important

- <u>fold</u> (bend) --- to bend something so that it touches itself

- <u>fire</u> (from a job) --- to make somebody leave their job

- <u>come up</u> (appear) --- to happen

- <u>no-call, no-show</u> --- not going to work and not telling your boss about it

- <u>inexcusable</u> --- so bad that you cannot accept it

- <u>see</u> (understand) --- to understand

- <u>from time to time</u> --- sometimes

- <u>hungover</u> --- feeling sick from drinking too much alcohol the day before

- <u>call in</u> (sick) --- to call your boss and tell them you are too sick to work

- <u>lenient</u> --- not strict

- <u>reliable</u> --- can be trusted

- <u>run</u> (business) --- to do or manage

- <u>remind</u> --- to help someone remember something

- <u>get on somebody's bad side</u> --- to do something to make sb. angry

- <u>promote</u> (job) --- to move someone to a bigger job

- <u>honestly</u> (truly) --- used to say what you are saying is true

- <u>mental</u> --- about the mind

- <u>time off</u> --- not working on days you normally work

Comprehension Questions

1. What is a "no-call, no-show"?
    A. An employee being fired
    B. An employee's absence from work without notifying the employer
    C. An unwritten rule at a workplace
    D. A rule forbidding the use of smartphones in the workplace

2. What is the opposite of "lenient"?
    A. Strict
    B. Straight
    C. Smart
    D. Supreme

3. Why does Lucy want to hire a second manager?
    A. She wants to be able to compete with the other local pizza delivery stores.
    B. She wants to be promoted.
    C. She wants to quit.
    D. She wants to take time off work for her mental health.

CHAPTER 5:
CHATTING WITH CLASSMATES

(Charlie is at school attending an <u>economics</u> <u>lecture</u>.)

Professor: <u>That will be it</u> for today. Don't forget to study for the <u>upcoming</u> <u>midterm</u>. For every hour you spend here, you should spend at least two hours <u>reviewing</u>.

(The students start <u>packing up</u> their <u>belongings</u> and leaving the lecture <u>hall</u>. A student to the left of Charlie starts up a conversation.)

Classmate: Two hours? That's way too much! We all have lives, <u>you know?</u>
Charlie: Yeah, it's a lot.
Classmate: I <u>get</u> that we have to study to get a good grade and all, but <u>dude</u>.
Charlie: And it's an economics class, which most people here are not <u>majoring in</u>. What major are you?
Classmate: <u>Engineering</u>. You?
Charlie: Undecided, so I'm <u>kind of</u> just <u>floating around</u> for now.
Classmate: I see. Yeah, there's so much going on <u>campus</u> every single day. Did you hear about the 48-hour film festival coming up this weekend?
Charlie: That's the one where each team has 48 hours to make a movie, right? I did hear about that. Are you going?

Classmate: Sure am. Gonna enter with some friends and see what happens. How about you?

Charlie: <u>Nah</u>, I can't do anything film-<u>related</u> at all. I'm not even sure I would last 48 seconds before <u>screwing something up</u>. I have been thinking about <u>taking up</u> cooking classes, <u>though</u>.

Vocabulary

- <u>economics</u> --- the study of how money is made and used

- <u>lecture</u> (education) --- a talk to teach a subject to a group of people

- <u>that will be it</u> --- used when you want to stop something

- <u>upcoming</u> --- happening soon

- <u>midterm</u> --- a test given in the middle of a school course

- <u>review</u> (study) --- to look again at something you studied before

- <u>pack up</u> --- to collect all of your things after finishing something

- <u>belongings</u> --- things you own and carry around

- <u>hall</u> (large place) --- a large room or building for events

- <u>you know?</u> --- *(informal)* used when what you are saying is known

- <u>get</u> (understand) --- *(informal)* to understand

- <u>dude</u> [interjection] --- *(slang)* used to show strong feelings

- <u>major in</u> --- to study something as your main subject in college

- <u>engineering</u> --- the science of designing and building things

- <u>kind of</u> --- *(informal)* a little

- float around [idiom] --- to not be in any exact place

- campus --- the buildings and land inside a college

- nah --- *(informal)* no

- related (connected) --- connected

- screw something up (fail) --- to do something badly

- take up something (start) --- to start doing something

- though --- while, but

Comprehension Questions

1. According to the professor, if you spent 10 hours in class, how many hours should you review for the midterm?
   A. 10 hours
   B. 15 hours
   C. 20 hours
   D. 25 hours

2. Which of the following is NOT a college major?
   A. Undecided
   B. Economics
   C. Engineering
   D. Studying

3. What happens at a 48-hour film festival?
    A. People gather in a large theater to watch films for 48 hours straight.
    B. People gather to watch the premiere of a new movie that is 48 hours in length.
    C. Teams enter to create and compete for the best film in under 48 hours.
    D. Teams enter a 48-hour ultra-marathon race and capture it on film.

CHAPTER 6:

THE SECRET INGREDIENT

(Charlie attends an evening cooking class <u>located</u> inside the student center on campus.)

Instructor: The onions are the most important part of this recipe. They have to be <u>seasoned</u> <u>properly</u>, or the curry will not have as much <u>flavor</u>.

Student #1: So, you add salt, pepper, garlic, and <u>ginger</u> when cooking the onions?

Instructor: Yes, and now comes the secret <u>ingredient</u>.

Student #2: What's the secret ingredient?

Instructor: It wouldn't be a secret anymore if I told you.

Charlie: But how <u>are we supposed to</u> make this dish at home?

Instructor: The person who guesses the secret ingredient gets a prize!

Student #1: OK. Is it <u>coconut</u>?

Instructor: No.

Student #2: How about <u>olive</u> oil?

Instructor: Try again.

Charlie: Is it love?

Instructor: That's the secret ingredient in everything, so <u>nope</u>.

Student #1: Ice cream?

(The instructor <u>coldly</u> <u>stares</u> at Student #1.)

Charlie: I think he means to say that we all give up.

Instructor: Very well then. The correct answer is basil. And since no one guessed right, it looks like I will be keeping the prize to enjoy all by myself.

seasoned performer/traveller 经验丰富表演家旅行家

The sausage was very highly seasoned 这香肠调味很浓

Vocabulary

- locate (be) --- to be in an exact place

- season [verb] --- to add salt, pepper, and other spices to food

- properly (correctly) --- correctly

- flavor (taste) --- how food or drink tastes

- ginger (spice) --- a spicy root used in cooking

- ingredient --- one of many things used to make something

- be supposed to (expect) --- to be expected to do or be something

- coconut --- a large brown hard fruit with a white inside

- olive --- a small green or black fruit with a very hard center

- nope --- *(informal)* no

- coldly --- in an unfriendly way

- stare --- to look at something for a long time

- very well --- used to say you agree or accept something

- basil --- a plant with sweet leaves that and are used for cooking

- (all) by myself --- alone

Comprehension Questions

1. What does the instructor season the onions with?
   A. Salt, pepper, garlic, and ginger
   B. Salt, pepper, and olive oil
   C. Salt, pepper, and coconut oil
   D. Ice cream

2. Where is the cooking class located?
   A. Inside the student center off campus
   B. Inside a lecture hall
   C. Outside the student center off campus
   D. Inside the student center on campus

3. What was the prize for guessing the secret ingredient?
   A. Basil
   B. Cash
   C. Ice cream
   D. Unknown

CHAPTER 7:
A DATE WITH A STRANGER

(Charlie has met someone online through a dating app. After chatting for a few days, they agree to meet <u>in person</u> for a date at a local coffee shop.)

Charlie: Hi, are you Angela?
Angela: Yes. Hi.
Charlie: I'm Charlie. Nice to meet you.
Angela: Nice to meet you, too.
Charlie: You look a lot cuter in person.
Angela: Oh, thanks. You, too.
Charlie: So, uh, do you come to this coffee shop a lot?
Angela: Yeah, sometimes.
Charlie: When?
Angela: After school.
Charlie: Oh, that's cool. What is your major?
Angela: <u>Computer science</u>.
Charlie: How's that <u>working out</u> for you?
Angela: It's kind of fun, I guess.
Charlie: What <u>got you into</u> that?
Angela: Um, well, it pays pretty well.
Charlie: It does, doesn't it?
Angela: <u>Yup</u>.
Charlie: You <u>gotta</u> love jobs that pay you good money.

Angela: <u>Mm-hmm</u>.

(The two sit in <u>awkward</u> <u>silence</u> for <u>roughly</u> 10 seconds.)

Angela: Oh. Uh, I just got a text from a friend. I think I should go meet them.
Charlie: Oh, OK. Well, it was nice meeting you.

(Angela picks up her belongings and leaves the coffee shop. Charlie immediately takes out his smartphone and starts to <u>ponder</u> what <u>went wrong</u>.)

Vocabulary

- <u>stranger</u> --- someone you don't know

- <u>in person</u> --- by meeting someone

- <u>computer science</u> --- the study of computers

- <u>work out</u> (happen) --- to happen or develop

- <u>get into</u> (start) --- to start being involved or interested in sth.

- <u>yup</u> --- (informal) yes

- <u>gotta</u> --- *(informal)* have got to, have got a

- <u>mm-hmm</u> --- used to agree or show lack of interest

- <u>awkward</u> (embarrassed) --- makes you feel embarrassed

- <u>silence</u> --- no sound at all

- <u>roughly</u> --- close to but not exactly

- <u>ponder</u> --- to think carefully about something

- <u>go wrong</u> --- to have a problem, to make a mistake

Comprehension Questions

1. Where did Charlie first meet Angela?
   A. At the cooking class
   B. During one of his classes
   C. They both work at the same pizza delivery place.
   D. Through an online dating app

2. How would you describe the general tone of the conversation in this chapter?
   A. Awkward
   B. Serious
   C. Arrogant
   D. Intimate

3. When will the second date between Charlie and Angela occur?
   A. When Charlie gets his next paycheck
   B. Sometime during the weekend
   C. When the semester ends
   D. There probably won't be a second date.

CHAPTER 8:

PUMPING IRON

(Charlie has decided to start working out at the college gym on campus. He is just about to start lifting <u>weights</u> when he decides to ask for help.)

Charlie: Excuse me. Sorry to <u>bother</u> you.

Stranger: No problem. What can I do for you?

Charlie: I just started weight training today, and I was <u>wondering</u>, how did you get so <u>lean</u> and <u>shredded</u>? It's really <u>impressive</u>.

Stranger: Oh, uh, thanks. It takes hard work and time just like anything else.

Charlie: <u>Let's say</u> you had eight weeks to <u>get into shape</u> starting <u>from scratch</u>. What would you do?

Stranger: Well, you're going to get pretty <u>limited</u> results if you work out for only eight weeks. The <u>fitness</u> <u>industry</u> would have you believe that you can get a professional model's <u>physique</u> in eight weeks if you just buy what they are selling.

Charlie: I don't know. I've seen a lot of amazing before-and-after photos.

Stranger: That's another <u>trick</u>. Those paid actors already had a lot of <u>muscle</u> on them before they went on a diet to <u>cut</u> all the fat.

Charlie: Alright then. What kind of eight week program would you recommend for a beginner?

Stranger: <u>I'll tell you what</u>. If you start with the <u>basics</u> and do heavy <u>squats</u>, <u>deadlifts</u>, and <u>bench presses</u>, you'll see some very real <u>strength</u> and size <u>gains</u>.

Charlie: OK. Can you show me which machines I use for those?

Stranger: These are <u>barbell</u> exercises. You'll get <u>triple</u> the gains if you train with the barbell.

Charlie: I don't know. That seems pretty hard.

Stranger: It's supposed to be. That's exactly how you get big and strong.

Charlie: I'll <u>keep that in mind</u>. What would you do diet-<u>wise</u>?

Stranger: You're going to want to eat a small <u>calorie surplus</u> that's about 200-300 calories above what you normally eat. And not <u>junk food</u> but <u>nutritious</u> food that's also high in <u>protein</u>.

Charlie: Do you mean I have to count calories?

Stranger: You don't have to <u>necessarily</u>. Start by cutting all junk food from your diet and replacing it with lots of healthy foods.

Charlie: OK, I see. I really <u>appreciate</u> the help. I'll <u>see</u> what I can do.

(<u>Overwhelmed</u> by the information given to him by the stranger, Charlie decides to go for a run on the <u>treadmill</u> instead.)

Vocabulary

- <u>pump iron</u> --- *(informal)* to lift heavy weights for exercise

- <u>weights</u> --- heavy things

- <u>bother</u> (worry) --- to make someone angry or worried

- <u>wonder</u> (request) --- used as a polite way to ask a question

- <u>lean</u> (no fat) --- little to no fat

- <u>shredded</u> --- *(informal)* having big muscles and little body fat

- <u>impressive</u> --- making you admire something

- <u>(let's) say</u> --- used to introduce an idea

- <u>get into shape</u> --- to become fit through exercise and diet

- <u>from scratch</u> --- from the beginning with nothing

- <u>limited</u> (small) --- small in amount

- <u>fitness</u> (health) --- being healthy and strong

- <u>industry</u> (business) --- the people and companies in one type of business

- <u>physique</u> --- the shape and size of a person's body

- <u>trick</u> (trap) --- something you do to make someone believe sth.

- <u>muscle</u> (body) --- a part of the body that makes the body move

- <u>cut</u> (reduce) --- to make something smaller

- <u>I'll tell you what</u> --- used to introduce an idea

- <u>basics</u> --- the simplest and most important things

- <u>squats</u> --- an exercise where you bend you legs and then stand up straight

- <u>deadlifts</u> --- an exercise where you pick up a weight from the floor

- <u>bench presses</u> --- an exercise where you lie on a bench and push a weight

- <u>strength</u> (power) --- being strong

- <u>gains</u> --- increases in something

- <u>barbell</u> --- a long metal bar with weights on the ends

- <u>triple</u> --- three times

- <u>keep something in mind</u> --- to remember something

- <u>-wise</u> --- about

- <u>calorie</u> --- a number for how much energy is in a food

- <u>surplus</u> --- an extra amount

- <u>junk food</u> --- food that is bad for your health

- <u>nutritious</u> --- *(of food)* good for your health

- <u>protein</u> --- a thing found in meat, beans, and nuts that you need to be healthy

- <u>necessarily</u> (therefore) --- in every case

- <u>appreciate</u> (be grateful) --- used to thank someone

- <u>see</u> (find out) --- to find out

- <u>overwhelm</u> (feel) --- to make someone feel too much of sth.

- <u>treadmill</u> --- an exercise machine you walk and run on

Comprehension Questions

1. Which of the following most accurately describes the stranger's physique?
    A. Massive and bulky
    B. Slim and muscular
    C. Frail and skinny
    D. Fluffy and flabby

2. What does it mean "to get into shape"?
    A. To become physically more fit through exercise
    B. To bend something into a particular shape so that it fits into something else
    C. To become a shapeshifter
    D. To bend one's body to perform certain exercises

3. The stranger recommends that Charlie do all the following EXCEPT...
    A. Eat nutritious foods at a caloric surplus
    B. Eat junk foods at a caloric deficit
    C. Cut out all junk foods
    D. Do barbell exercises

CHAPTER 9:

THE LATEST TREND

(Charlie goes over to Ben's house to hang out for the night.)

[handwritten annotations: He hangs out in an old house 居住; hang out at McDonald's when it started to rain; 泡芙]

Ben: So, how did that date go this week with that girl?

Charlie: Terrible. It didn't last longer than three minutes.

Ben: Ouch. Was it one of those dates where it was immediately awkward?

Charlie: Pretty much. I'm thinking it's because of the way I look, but you never know, right?

Ben: At least you're putting yourself out there. You're bound to find someone if you keep trying.

Charlie: What about you? I know you're low on money but...

Ben: You just answered your own question.

Charlie: How's the job hunt coming along?

Ben: Good. Hey, did you hear about the announcement today?

Charlie: No. What was it?

Ben: They announced the new RPG today. It looks absolutely insane. They even hired a few A-list celebrities to do the voice acting. The hype surrounding this game is unreal. I pre-ordered it immediately after the press event ended.

Charlie: The internet is always on fire over something. I still haven't played the big game that came out this year. It's like, as soon I finish one game, 10 more pop up that people are telling me to play. I just can't keep up.

Ben: I can.

Charlie: How?

Ben: Easy. Don't have a life. Do that and suddenly you have all the time <u>in the world</u>. Problem solved.

Vocabulary

- <u>latest</u> --- newest

- <u>trend</u> [noun] --- a change in people or in a situation

- <u>ouch</u> --- used to say something hurts

- <u>pretty much</u> --- *(informal)* almost completely

- <u>put yourself out there</u> --- to make an effort to do something

- <u>bound</u> (certain) --- certain to happen

- <u>job hunt</u> --- job search

- <u>come along</u> (develop) --- to develop

- <u>announcement</u> --- a statement someone makes to everybody

- <u>RPG</u> --- a type of game where players become characters in a story

- <u>absolutely</u> --- in every way

- <u>insane</u> (good) --- *(informal)* extremely good

- <u>hire</u> --- to give someone a job

- <u>A-list</u> --- the most famous people

- <u>celebrities</u> --- famous people

- <u>hype</u> --- a very large amount of excitement for something new

- surrounding --- everywhere around something

- unreal (surprising) --- *(informal)* extremely good or surprising

- pre-order [verb] --- to order something before it is available

- press (news) --- the people and companies that report the news

- on fire (excited) --- very excited about something

- come out (release) --- to become available to the public

- like (pause) --- *(informal)* used when you are thinking of what to say

✓ • pop up --- to appear suddenly

✓ • keep up --- to continue to do something at a high level

- in the world --- used to show what you are saying is important

Comprehension Questions

1. What does it mean "to put oneself out there?"
   A. To go outside
   B. To escape danger
   C. To make a considerable effort
   D. To put oneself into a dangerous situation

2. What is an "A-list celebrity?"
   A. A celebrity currently at the top of their career
   B. A celebrity who appears on a list
   C. A celebrity who got high test grades in school
   D. A celebration of celebrities

3. What does it mean "to not have a life?"
  A. To be dead
  B. To be unconscious
  C. To use up all of your player lives in a video game
  D. To spend all of one's time doing nothing significant or meaningful

CHAPTER 10:
THE MEANING OF SACRIFICE

(Charlie is at work chatting with Lucy while folding pizza boxes.)

Lucy: We have a lot of <u>deliveries coming up</u> tonight. It's going to be a busy night. I like it when it's busy. It means that <u>time flies</u>, and we get home <u>before you know it</u>.

Charlie: I heard you have a son. How old is he?

Lucy: He just <u>turned</u> 15 <u>the other day</u>.

Charlie: So, he stays home with his dad while you're here in the evening?

Lucy: <u>Honey</u>, he has a father but not a dad.

Charlie: So, you <u>raised</u> him all by yourself?

Lucy: I did. Of course, my son doesn't <u>see</u> it that way. I had to go to work almost every day to pay our bills, so we didn't get to spend too much time together. My mom, his grandmother, is the one who <u>looked after</u> him while I worked.

Charlie: But now he is old enough to stay home alone, right?

Lucy: Yes. It's good for my mom, who needed the break, but now he's <u>lonely</u>, you know?

Charlie: That's <u>rough</u>.

Lucy: We <u>compete</u> with two other pizza delivery places, and it <u>takes</u> everything I have just to keep this place <u>in business</u>. If I take even a <u>day off</u>, I get a call from the owner, and he never calls <u>unless</u> it's something bad.

Charlie: Wow, that's a lot to deal with. If it makes you feel any better, one day he will <u>look back</u> and realize how much his mom <u>sacrificed</u> for him.

Lucy: Can that day be today, please?

Vocabulary

- <u>time flies</u> --- used to say that time passes very quickly

- <u>before somebody knows it</u> --- surprisingly quickly

- <u>turn</u> (become) --- to become

- <u>the other day</u> --- recently

- <u>honey</u> (the South) --- *(informal)* a name used by women in the Southern US

- <u>raise</u> (care) --- to care for a child or animal until they are fully grown

- <u>see</u> (consider) --- to think about

- <u>look after</u> --- to take care of something

- <u>lonely</u> (feeling) --- unhappy because you are alone

- <u>rough</u> (difficult) --- difficult

- <u>compete</u> --- to try to be better than someone

- <u>take</u> (need) --- to need

- <u>in business</u> --- used to say a business is working

- <u>day off</u> --- a day you don't work

- <u>unless</u> --- except when

- <u>look back</u> --- to think about something in the past

- <u>sacrifice</u> [verb] --- to give up sth. important to have sth. more important

Comprehension Questions

1. Why does Lucy like busy nights?
   A. She makes the most money on those nights.
   B. Time goes by quickly, which means everyone gets to go home sooner.
   C. The owner comes to visit.
   D. It means that there will be a celebration party after work.

2. How was Lucy's son raised?
   A. By Lucy and her husband who worked all the time
   B. By Lucy, who worked all the time and by Lucy's mother, who watched over him at home
   C. By foster parents who watched over him at home
   D. By an orphanage

3. What happens if Lucy takes a day off?
   A. The pizza shop will catch on fire.
   B. The employees will protest.
   C. The owner will call her up and scold her.
   D. The customers won't order any food.

CHAPTER 11:
CHATTING WITH CUSTOMERS

(Charlie is out on a delivery. He arrives at the customer's apartment and rings the <u>doorbell</u> with the order in hand. A <u>middle-aged</u> man opens the door.)

Charlie: Hi there. I have a <u>pineapple</u> pizza for apartment 312.
Customer: That's me. Here's the money for the order. You can keep the <u>change</u>.
Charlie: Thank you.
Customer: You look like you're a student in college. Am I right?
Charlie: Yes, sir.
Customer: Best four years of my life right there. <u>Live it up</u> while you can because those <u>golden years</u> will be gone before you know it.
Charlie: <u>I will certainly try.</u>
Customer: What do you study?
Charlie: I did chemistry for a bit, but now I'm not sure what I want to do.
Customer: Don't worry about that. You have your whole life to figure that out. You're young. Just enjoy the college life. Parties, drinking, new friends, and the women!
Charlie: I will! Oh, by the way, if you don't mind me asking, what did you study?
Customer: History. Although it did me no good in the end. I couldn't find a job after <u>graduation</u>, so now I'm a delivery driver too, actually.

Vocabulary

- <u>doorbell</u> --- a button you push to let people inside know you are outside

- <u>middle-aged</u> --- between the ages 40 to 65

- <u>pineapple</u> --- a large fruit with a hard skin and a sweet yellow inside

- <u>change</u> (money) --- small amounts of money

- <u>live it up</u> --- to enjoy parties and good food and drink

- <u>golden years</u> --- the best years of your life

- <u>graduation</u> (completion) --- completing school or college

Comprehension Questions

1. How did the customer pay for the pizza?
    A. By credit card
    B. By check
    C. By cash
    D. By money order

2. What was the customer's advice to Charlie?
    A. Don't worry so much about his college major and instead party it up.
    B. Get into a long-term relationship quickly, settle down, and get married.
    C. Focus all of his attention and time on his studies.
    D. Focus on accumulating as much money as he can, so he can start preparing for his future.

3. What was the customer's problem with studying history?
    A. He found it too boring.
    B. He found that the jobs relating to history didn't pay as much as he wanted.
    C. He couldn't find a job after graduating.
    D. He dropped out of college.

CHAPTER 12:
CHECKING OUT BOOKS

(Charlie is at the library on campus, looking for an <u>inspiring</u> book. He finds a book that he would like to read and goes to <u>check it out</u>.)

Charlie: Hi, I'd like to check out this book.
Librarian: OK. Do you have your student <u>ID card</u>?
Charlie: Yes. Here you go.
Librarian: All right. Let me just put this book <u>under your name</u>.

(A few moments of silence pass.)

Charlie: Hey, have you ever read anything by the author of this book?
Librarian: Can't say that I have. What kind of author is he?
Charlie: I've heard that he writes about the lives of people who have <u>made history</u>. So many people have recommended his books to me because of the <u>practical</u> <u>wisdom</u> they <u>contain</u>.
Librarian: Oh, that does sound good. I'm more of a <u>fiction</u> reader. I think all great stories have some <u>underlying</u> wisdom in them. But what I like about fiction is that <u>it's up to</u> the reader to find and <u>interpret</u> that life <u>lesson</u> for themselves.
Charlie: For me, because of school, I've always <u>associated</u> reading novels with <u>boredom</u>.
Librarian: So, that's why you read <u>non-fiction</u>?

Charlie: I don't really read much at all. This is the first book I've picked up outside school.

Vocabulary

- <u>inspiring</u> --- making you feel you want to do something

- <u>check something out</u> (borrow) --- to borrow sth. from a library

- <u>librarian</u> --- a person who works at a library

- <u>ID card</u> --- a card with information that shows who you are

- <u>under someone's name</u> --- used to say something belongs to sb.

- <u>make history</u> --- to do sth. so important that it will be recorded in history

- <u>practical</u> (real) --- actually doing sth. rather than thinking about it

- <u>wisdom</u> --- the power to make smart decisions

- <u>contain</u> --- to have something inside

- <u>fiction</u> --- a story that is created and not real

- <u>underlying</u> (hidden) --- real but not immediately noticed

- <u>be up to somebody</u> --- to be somebody's job to decide or deal with

- <u>interpret</u> (decide) --- to decide the meaning of something

- <u>lesson</u> (experience) --- an experience you learn from

- <u>associate</u> (connect) --- to connect two things in your mind

- <u>boredom</u> --- being bored

- <u>non-fiction</u> --- writing that is about real things and people

Comprehension Questions

1. What do you need in order to check out a book from the college library?
    A. A student ID card
    B. Money
    C. A driver's license
    D. A state ID

2. What does the author of the book Charlie is interested in write about?
    A. About the lives of librarians
    B. About the lives of people who have made history
    C. About the history of practical wisdom
    D. About the history of people and the world

3. Why does the librarian prefer fiction?
    A. It's more fun and exciting than non-fiction.
    ✓ B. It's up to the reader to find the wisdom and life lessons contained within the story.
    C. It has fantasy, sci-fi, and romance novels.
    D. It's overall wiser to read fiction than non-fiction.

CHAPTER 13:
FAMILY TIME

(Charlie is lying on the couch in the living room of his apartment, enjoying his new book, when his mom comes back from grocery shopping.)

Mom: Hey, Charlie.

Charlie: Welcome back.

Mom: Thanks. The new grocery store here is so cheap. I love it!

Charlie: Oh yeah? What did you buy?

Mom: I got all our vegetables at half price. There's fresh radishes, pumpkins, and cabbage. I also got fruits for pretty cheap. We have apples, strawberries, and blueberries.

Charlie: That sounds great. What are we having for dinner tonight?

Mom: I was actually thinking about getting take-out tonight. How does soup and sandwiches sound?

Charlie: I'd love some.

Mom: My pleasure. By the way, what class is that book for?

Charlie: It's not for class. I got it at the library.

Mom: Oh. Have you finished studying for the day?

Charlie: Mom, I don't even know what I want to study.

Mom: I thought you were doing chemistry.

Charlie: Nah. I dropped it. I changed my major to undecided for now.

Mom: Well, it's good that you're keeping your brain sharp. What do you think about doing something else science-related?

Charlie: Chemistry was the science I liked best, but I'm not sure it's my true passion anymore.

(Charlie <u>buries</u> his face into his book.)

Charlie: Why can't I just know what I want?
Mom: There's a really good <u>quote</u> by <u>Bruce Lee</u> that I love. "<u>Pray</u> not for an easy life. Pray for the strength to <u>endure</u> a difficult one."

Vocabulary

- <u>grocery shopping</u> --- food shopping

- <u>Oh yeah?</u> --- *(informal)* used to say "Is that so?"

- <u>radishes</u> --- small round red vegetables with a white inside

- <u>pumpkins</u> --- large round orange vegetables

- <u>cabbage</u> --- a round vegetable with large green, purple, or white leaves

- <u>take-out</u> --- a meal you buy at a restaurant and eat somewhere else

- <u>my pleasure</u> --- a polite way to reply to someone thanking you

- <u>drop</u> (stop) --- to stop doing something

- <u>sharp</u> (intelligent) --- clever or quick to notice things

- <u>bury</u> (hide) --- to hide something

- <u>quote</u> (words) --- words someone has said or written

- <u>Bruce Lee</u> --- a famous actor and martial artist from Hong Kong

- <u>pray</u> (hope) --- to hope very much for sth.

• <u>endure</u> (experience) --- to experience sth. difficult and not give up

Comprehension Questions

1. What did Charlie's mom say that she bought at the grocery store?
    A. Ramen, pickles, cucumbers, apricots, sundaes, and bananas
    B. Rice, pizza, carrots, acorns, salads, and bagels
    C. Relish, pineapples, cake, asparagus, sandwiches, and bacon
    D. Radishes, pumpkins, cabbage, apples, strawberries, and blueberries

2. What will Charlie and his mom eat for dinner tonight?
    A. They will make soup and sandwiches at home.
    B. They will get soup and sandwiches from a take-out restaurant.
    C. They will eat soup and sandwiches inside a local restaurant.
    D. They will go to a friend's house for soup and sandwiches.

3. Which of the following fields of study is NOT science-related?
    A. Chemistry
    B. Physics
    C. Biology
    D. Cryptology

CHAPTER 14:

THE DEFINITION OF GENIUS

(Charlie and Ben are having drinks in a local bar.)

Ben: What do you mean there's no such thing as a genius?

Charlie: What we call genius is just someone who has figured out what their natural talents are and has spent over 10 years perfecting them. People see only the end result and none of the hard work, so it's just easy to call it genius.

Ben: But what about Mozart? Wasn't he a child prodigy?

Charlie: That's a great example. What people don't consider is that he had shown a very high level of interest in music from a very early age. And his father was a professional musician, composer, conductor, and teacher. By the time Mozart turned three, he was receiving professional-level piano lessons all day, every day from his dad. At night, his parents had to pry him away from the piano just to get him to sleep.

Ben: Hmm, I don't know. How can you believe that there's no such thing as a genius? Where are you getting this argument from?

Charlie: From a book.

Ben: You would believe something you read in a single book?

Charlie: Well, I've heard this argument elsewhere, too. As humans, we don't want to come to terms with our personal failures and mistakes, so it's easier to look at successful people and call them lucky, gifted, or genius.

Ben: <u>Whoa</u>, now. Are you saying people don't get lucky? What about <u>incredibly</u> <u>competitive</u> <u>fields</u> like acting or YouTube?

Charlie: Luck is definitely a <u>factor</u>, <u>no doubt</u>. What I'm saying is that if you want more luck, you gotta <u>take more chances</u>.

(While Charlie is talking, Ben looks over Charlie's shoulder and <u>spots</u> two attractive girls sitting at another table.)

Ben: Speaking of taking more chances, I see some across the room right now. Follow me.

Vocabulary

- <u>definition</u> --- the explanation of the meaning of a word or phrase

- <u>there's no such thing</u> --- used to say that something doesn't exist

- <u>genius</u> (person) --- sb. who is extremely intelligent, skilled, or creative

- <u>call</u> (consider) --- to consider something to be something

- <u>talents</u> (abilities) --- natural abilities to do something well

- <u>perfect</u> [verb] --- to make something as perfect as possible

- <u>prodigy</u> --- a young genius

- <u>composer</u> --- a person who writes music

- <u>conductor</u> (music) --- a person who leads musicians or singers

- <u>get</u> (convince) --- to make or convince somebody do sth.

- <u>argument</u> (reasons) --- the reasons why you agree or disagree with an idea

- <u>elsewhere</u> --- somewhere else

- <u>come to terms with sth.</u> --- to learn to accept a sad situation

- <u>failures</u> (not successful) --- things that did not succeed

- <u>gifted</u> --- having a lot of intelligence or natural ability

- <u>whoa</u> (surprised) --- used to show surprise or interest

- <u>incredibly</u> (extremely) --- extremely

- <u>competitive</u> --- trying to be better than others

- <u>fields</u> (subjects) --- types of different work or interests

- <u>factor</u> (cause) --- one of many things that causes something

- <u>no doubt</u> --- certainly

- <u>take chances</u> --- to do things that could have good or bad results

- <u>spot</u> (see) --- to notice something that isn't easily seen

Comprehension Questions

1. How does Charlie define what a "genius" is?
    A. Someone who is incredibly intelligent and skilled
    B. Someone who invents something revolutionary
    C. Someone who has figured out their natural talents and spent over 10 years perfecting them
    D. Someone who has spent over 10 years searching for their natural talents

2. What is another word for "genius"?
    A. Intellectual
    B. Perfect
    C. Prodigy
    D. Professional

3. According to Charlie, "if you want more luck...
    A. you have to roll the dice."
    B. you have to get lucky."
    C. you have to take more chances."
    D. you have to find a horseshoe or four-leaf clover."

CHAPTER 15:
FILLING A PRESCRIPTION

(Charlie is at his local <u>pharmacy</u> to pick up some new medicine.)

Charlie: Hi, I'm here to pick up my <u>prescription</u>.
Pharmacist: OK. What's your name?
Charlie: Charlie Cash.
Pharmacist: And your date of birth?
Charlie: February 20, 2000.
Pharmacist: OK. Great. I'll be right back.

(The pharmacist goes to <u>retrieve</u> Charlie's prescription.)

Pharmacist: Alright. Do you have any questions about taking this <u>medication</u>?
Charlie: Yes. I take it in the morning and evening, right?
Pharmacist: That's right.
Charlie: Do I take it with food or can I take it on an empty stomach?
Pharmacist: Either is fine.
Charlie: I see. How about if I take the medication at different times during the day? My <u>schedule</u> changes all the time <u>due to</u> work and school.
Pharmacist: <u>As long as</u> each <u>dose</u> is taken sometime during the morning and sometime during the evening, you'll be fine.

Charlie: OK, thank you. Wait! I forgot to ask one last thing. I swallow the pill, right? Or is it chewable?
Pharmacist: You have to swallow it. You can't chew it. Other than that, can I assist you with anything?
Charlie: Yes. Where's the water fountain? I need to take it as soon as possible.

Vocabulary

- fill a prescription --- to prepare a medicine at a pharmacy to take home

- pharmacy --- a store that sells medicine

- prescription --- a written order from a doctor for a medicine

- pharmacist --- the person who prepares medicine at the pharmacy

- retrieve --- to go find something and bring it back

- medication --- one or more medicines

- schedule [noun] --- a plan of things with times they will happen

- due to (caused by) --- because of

- as long as (only if) --- only if

- dose (of medicine) --- an amount of medicine taken at one time

- swallow (eat) --- to make sth. go from your mouth to your stomach

- pill --- a small piece of medicine you take by swallowing

- chewable --- can be chewed *(cut into smaller pieces with your teeth)*

- other than --- except

- <u>assist</u> --- *(formal)* to help

- <u>water fountain</u> --- a machine you drink water from

- <u>as soon as possible</u> --- as quickly as you can

Comprehension Questions

1. Where do you go to pick up prescriptions?
   - A. Pharmacy
   - B. Doctor's office
   - C. School
   - D. Workplace

2. Should Charlie take his medication with or without food?
   - A. With food.
   - B. Without food.
   - C. It doesn't matter.
   - D. It depends on the situation.

3. Which of the following is NOT an oral administration of medication?
   - A. Injecting
   - B. Swallowing
   - C. Chewing
   - D. Drinking

CHAPTER 16:

INTERVIEW WITH A WITNESS

(Charlie is at home watching the local news on TV.)

Newscaster: Authorities say that the suspect's whereabouts are still unknown. What we do know is that the suspect is male, aged 18-35, and approximately five feet 10 inches tall. We go now to an interview with a bystander who was a witness at the scene.

(The camera cuts to a news correspondent and a middle-aged woman.)

Reporter: Can you briefly summarize what you saw?
Witness: I was walking home from work when I noticed someone was dancing wildly at the intersection just up ahead. As I got closer to the intersection, I saw that they were wearing a large horse mask and had stripped down to their underwear. I thought I had taken crazy pills or something, but no, that actually happened today.
Reporter: How long did this person continue?
Witness: From the time I noticed him, I would say about a full minute.
Reporter: What happened after that?
Witness: He took a quick bow and then ran down the street. No more than 30 seconds later, a few cop cars showed up with their sirens blazing loud.

(The camera cuts back to the <u>news anchor</u> in the <u>studio</u>.)

Newscaster: This <u>marks</u> the masked dancer's third <u>appearance</u> in the last few months. As with every appearance, several <u>breaking-and-entering</u> crimes have been reported near the masked man's show. Authorities <u>suspect</u> a <u>connection</u> between the events.

Vocabulary

- <u>newscaster</u> --- someone who reads the news on TV or radio

- <u>authorities</u> (state) --- the people who have responsibility over an area

- <u>suspect</u> [noun] --- a person believed to have done a crime

- <u>whereabouts</u> --- the place where something is 行蹤，下落

  B whereabouts do you feel the pain?

- <u>unknown</u> --- not known

- <u>approximately</u> --- close to but not exactly

- <u>inches</u> --- a number for how long sth. is (there are 12 inches in a foot)

- <u>bystander</u> --- someone who sees sth. happen they didn't cause

- <u>witness</u> (bystander) --- a bystander who talks about what they saw

- <u>scene</u> (crime) --- a place where something bad has happened

- <u>cut</u> [verb] (film) --- to move from one picture to the next in TV or film

- <u>correspondent</u> (news) --- sb. who reports the news from a far away place

  特派員，通信者

- <u>briefly</u> (words) --- in a few words

- <u>summarize</u> --- to say just the most important ideas about sth.

- <u>wildly</u> --- in a way that isn't controlled

- <u>intersection</u> --- the place where two or more roads cross

- <u>mask</u> --- something you wear on your face that covers it

- <u>strip</u> (clothes) --- to take off most or all of your or sb. else's clothes

- <u>underwear</u> --- clothes you wear under your pants *(and shirt if you are a girl)*

- <u>take crazy pills</u> --- *(informal)* used as a joke to say you can't believe sth. you see

- <u>bow</u> (bend) --- to bend your head or body down and forward

- <u>cop</u> --- a police officer

- <u>show up</u> (arrive) --- to arrive somewhere you are arranged to be

- <u>sirens</u> --- machines that make a very loud noise to warn people

- <u>blazing</u> (extremely) --- extreme(ly)

- <u>news anchor</u> --- the main news reader on a news program

- <u>studio</u> (recording) --- a room where video and sound is recorded

- <u>mark</u> (remember) --- to officially remember an important event

- <u>appearance</u> (arrival) --- a time when something appears in public

- <u>breaking and entering</u> --- the crime of illegally entering a building

- <u>suspect</u> (believe) --- to believe something is probably true

- <u>connection</u> (link) --- something that connects two or more things

Comprehension Questions

1. Which of the following is NOT a synonym for the word "reporter"?

    A. Newscaster

    B. Correspondent

    C. Journalist

    D. Witness

2. What attire was the masked dancer wearing?

    A. Underwear only

    B. Full tuxedo

    C. Business casual

    D. Semi-formal

3. Which of the following is a synonym for "breaking and entering"?

    A. Felony

    B. Burglary

    C. Arson

    D. Forgery

CHAPTER 17:
COMBINING FORCES

(Charlie is attending a world history lecture on campus.)

Professor: Don't forget that midterms are coming up in two weeks. This one test <u>counts</u> for 25 percent of your <u>total</u> <u>grade</u>. If you haven't started preparing for the test, the best time would be now. That will be all for today. Enjoy the rest of the afternoon.

(The students start packing up their belongings and <u>heading</u> for the exit. Another student <u>approaches</u> Charlie.)

Student #1: Hi there. Would you be interested in doing a study group to help prepare for the exam?
Charlie: Sure. How many do you have <u>so far</u>? *until now*
Student #1: Well, now that you're in, that makes two people.
Charlie: Oh, I see. Uh...
Student #1: Don't worry. All we have to do is <u>grab</u> a few more people before they leave.

(Charlie <u>nods</u>. The two students <u>split up</u> to find more members to add to their <u>newly formed</u> group.)

Charlie: Hello. Are you looking for a study group for the midterm?
Student #2: That actually sounds like a good idea. I'll join.
Charlie: OK, great. Now we just need a time and place.

(Charlie and four other students stand in a circle to arrange the meeting time and place.)

Student #1: I was thinking we could meet this Friday at 6 p.m. at the library. Does that sound good with everybody?

(The students nod in <u>agreement</u>, <u>exchange</u> <u>contact</u> information and split up <u>shortly after</u>.)

Vocabulary

- <u>combine forces</u> --- to start to work together to achieve a goal

- <u>count</u> (have value) --- to have value

- <u>total</u> [noun] --- the amount after you add two or more things

- <u>grade</u> (score) --- a letter or number to show how good sth. is

- <u>head</u> (move) --- to move in a direction

- <u>approach</u> (get near) --- to come closer to something

- <u>so far</u> --- until now

- <u>grab</u> (attract) --- to get somebody's attention

- <u>nod</u> [verb] --- to move your head up and down to show sth.

- <u>split up</u> (separate) --- to separate something into parts

- <u>newly</u> --- recently

- <u>form</u> (make) --- to make something

- <u>agreement</u> (opinion) --- sharing the same opinion with somebody

- <u>exchange</u> [verb] --- to give and receive something of the same type

- <u>contact</u> (communication) --- communicating with someone

- <u>shortly after</u> --- a short time after

Comprehension Questions

1. When does a midterm test usually occur during a semester?
    A. At the end of the term
    B. Around the middle of the term
    C. At the start of the term
    D. At any random point in time

2. How did the students form the study group?
    A. They asked and invited classmates at the end of class.
    B. They posted an advertisement on the bulletin board.
    C. They arranged groups through an online forum.
    D. They asked and invited other students at parties.

3. How will the students keep in touch?
    A. They stood in a circle and held hands.
    B. They exchanged contact information.
    C. They all live in the same apartment building.
    D. They nodded in agreement.

CHAPTER 18:
ORDERING LUNCH

(Charlie finds himself ordering a salad for lunch at the <u>food court</u> on campus.)

Employee: Hi. Welcome to Salad <u>Express</u>. What can I get you?

Charlie: Hello. I'd like to order a <u>garden salad</u>.

Employee: OK. Would you like <u>spinach</u> or <u>romaine</u> <u>lettuce</u>?

Charlie: I'll take romaine lettuce.

Employee: And which vegetables would you like on it?

Charlie: <u>Celery</u>, onion, peppers, and <u>cucumbers</u>, please.

Employee: OK. And would you like any other <u>toppings</u>?

Charlie: Yeah. Let's <u>go with</u> <u>cashews</u>, <u>raspberries</u>, <u>croutons</u>, and <u>tortilla strips</u>.

Employee: <u>You got it</u>. And which <u>dressing</u> can I get you?

Charlie: I'll have the low-calorie Italian, please.

Employee: Alright. Would you like any snacks or drinks with your order?

Charlie: I'll take a bag of chips and a <u>diet soda</u>. That will be it for me.

Employee: OK. Will this be <u>for here</u> or <u>to go</u>?

Charlie: For here.

(Charlie notices a large <u>gathering</u> of more than 100 students walking off together <u>in the distance</u>.)

Charlie: Hey, any <u>idea</u> what's going on with that crowd over there?
Employee: Oh, I'm not sure. My guess is that it <u>has something to do with</u> the <u>rally</u> on campus today.

Vocabulary

- <u>food court</u> --- an indoor area with many small restaurants and tables to eat at

- <u>express</u> (service) --- a service that works very quickly

- <u>garden salad</u> --- a salad containing mostly uncooked vegetables

- <u>spinach</u> --- a vegetable with big dark-green leaves

- <u>romaine</u> --- a type of lettuce with long, narrow leaves

- <u>lettuce</u> --- a vegetable with big green leaves usually eaten in salads

- <u>celery</u> --- a vegetable with long, light-green stalks *(sticks)*

- <u>cucumbers</u> --- long dark-green vegetables with a light-green inside

- <u>toppings</u> --- food you can put on top of a dish for taste or appearance

- <u>go with</u> (choose) --- to choose something

- <u>cashews</u> --- a type of nut that is small and curved

- <u>raspberries</u> --- a type of fruit that is small, soft, and red

- <u>croutons</u> --- small pieces of toasted bread used in soups and salads

- <u>tortilla strips</u> --- long, narrow corn chips

- <u>you got it</u> (agree) --- *(informal)* used to say you will do what sb. asks of you

- <u>dressing</u> --- a sauce you put on salads

- <u>diet soda</u> --- a zero calorie sweet drink that is fizzy *(has bubbles)*

- <u>for here</u> (food) --- used to say you want to eat inside the restaurant

- <u>to go</u> (food) --- used to say you want to eat outside of the restaurant

- <u>gathering</u> (meeting) --- a meeting of many people

- <u>in the distance</u> --- far away but you can still see or hear it

- <u>idea</u> (understanding) --- an understanding of something

- <u>have something to do with something</u> --- to be about something

- <u>rally</u> (meeting) --- a large public meeting of people who share an idea

Comprehension Questions

1. Which of the following are NOT considered vegetables?
    A. Celery, onion, peppers, and cucumbers
    B. Spinach, romaine lettuce, iceberg lettuce, and kale
    C. Potatoes, sweet potatoes, corn, and squash
    D. Olives, tomatoes, avocados, and pumpkins

2. Which of the following foods are typically considered nuts?
    A. Cashews, coconuts, and raisins
    B. Cashews, macadamia nuts, and croutons
    C. Cashews, olives, and walnuts
    D. Cashews, almonds, and peanuts

3. Which of the following best describes what a diet soda is?

    A. A smaller sized soda

    B. A beverage that causes weight loss

    C. A drink that is scientifically proven to better tasting than regular soda

    D. A carbonated beverage with little to no sugar, flavored with artificial sweeteners

CHAPTER 19:

RUNNING FOR PRESIDENT

(Charlie has decided to join the rally event on campus today. He's currently seated in a stadium with thousands of other students. The rally is for none other than presidential candidate Boris Johnson, who is making appearances all across the nation.)

Johnson: Let's move on to the Q and A segment of the event. I see that several long lines have already formed, but I can't promise that I'll be able to answer more than a dozen. OK, here we go. First is the gentleman here.
Student #1: Hi. I just wanted to ask something small. What's your morning routine look like? What do you do when you first get up?
Johnson: Well, when I first get up, I gotta pee just like everyone else.

(The audience chuckles.)

Johnson: After that, I spend the first 30 minutes with my personal assistant, whom I dearly love. I sip on a cup of coffee while she relays any new and relevant information to me. After that, we have a campaign staff meeting during which we review the day's upcoming events and our goals for each of them. When the meeting finishes, that's when I officially start the day. OK. Next question.

Student #2: Yes. I'm wondering, if you are <u>elected</u> as the next president, what will you do to help college students like me who are <u>struggling</u> <u>financially</u>?

Johnson: <u>Let me tell you</u> something you probably know. Students <u>have it worse</u> now than they have ever had it before! How can we expect the next <u>generation</u> to <u>lead</u> this nation if they can't even pay for their education? We have to start by <u>slashing</u> <u>tuition</u> costs and then <u>take it a step further</u> by creating new jobs for graduating students. And those who want to start a business <u>out of school</u> can't do so because <u>taxes</u> are too high. I think it's about time somebody lowered taxes for newly formed businesses!

(As the candidate finishes his answer, the audience <u>roars</u> with loud <u>cheers</u> and <u>applause</u>.)

Johnson: OK. Next.

Student #3: Can you tell us how you plan to cut tuition costs for students?

Johnson: Well, when I was a student way <u>back</u> 40 years ago, everyone could <u>afford</u> tuition. Back then, the government worked for the people and not the <u>corporations</u>. This <u>election</u> is all about putting the government back <u>in the hands of</u> the people. That's exactly what I will do if I'm elected. Next question!

Vocabulary

- <u>run</u> (for office) --- to become a candidate in an election

- <u>currently</u> --- now

- <u>seated</u> --- sitting

- <u>stadium</u> --- a very large building with many seats for big shows

- <u>none other than</u> --- used to say something as a surprise

- <u>presidential</u> --- connected to being the president

- <u>candidate</u> (job) --- a person who is trying to get elected or a job

- <u>nation</u> (country) --- a country

- <u>move on</u> (start) --- to start doing something new

- <u>Q and A</u> --- question and answer

- <u>segment</u> (part) --- a part of something

- <u>dozen</u> --- twelve

- <u>gentleman</u> (formality) --- *(formal)* used to talk politely to or about a man

- <u>pee</u> [verb] --- *(informal)* to remove urine from your body

- <u>chuckle</u> --- to laugh quietly

- <u>whom</u> --- the object form of "who"

- <u>dearly</u> --- very much

- <u>sip</u> [verb] --- to drink something a very small amount at a time

- <u>relay</u> (tell) --- to receive information and tell someone about it

- <u>relevant</u> --- connected to what is happening now

- <u>campaign</u> --- a group of planned actions designed to achieve sth.

- <u>staff</u> (workers) --- all the workers in an organization

- <u>officially</u> (publicly) --- publicly and by somebody with power

- <u>elect</u> (vote) --- to choose someone for a job by voting

- <u>struggle</u> (try hard) --- to try very hard to do something difficult

- <u>financially</u> --- in a way that is connected to money

- <u>let me tell you</u> --- used to say something important

- <u>have it bad</u> --- to have a difficult time

- <u>generation</u> (age) --- all the people who were born around the same time

- <u>lead</u> (control) --- to control a group of people

- <u>slash</u> (reduce) --- *(informal)* to reduce something by a lot

- <u>tuition</u> (money) --- money students pay colleges for teaching

- <u>take something further</u> --- to take a more serious action with sth.

- <u>out of school</u> --- not attending school

- <u>taxes</u> --- money that you have to pay the government

- <u>roar</u> (shout) --- to shout very loudly

- <u>cheers</u> (shouts) --- shouts of happiness or support

- <u>applause</u> --- the sound of people clapping

- <u>back</u> (past) --- in the past

- <u>afford</u> (have enough) --- to have the time or money to do sth.

- <u>corporations</u> (companies) --- very large companies

- <u>election</u> --- when people choose someone for a job by voting

- <u>in the hands of somebody</u> --- under control or care of somebody

Comprehension Questions

1. Complete the following sentence. A presidential candidate...
    A. is a person who has won the presidential election.
    B. is a person who was formerly president.
    C. is a person who is currently running for president.
    D. is a person who is currently serving as vice president.

2. How does Boris Johnson plan on helping college students who are struggling financially?
    A. He will increase tuition costs, create new jobs, and raise taxes for starting businesses.
    B. He will cut tuition costs, create new jobs, and cut taxes for starting businesses.
    C. He will raise tuition costs, cut new jobs, and increase taxes for starting businesses.
    D. He will decrease tuition costs, cut new jobs, and decrease taxes for starting businesses.

3. How exactly will Boris Johnson cut tuition costs?
    A. It's unclear how he will do so.
    B. He will increase taxes on the wealthy.
    C. He will issue government grants to colleges and universities.
    D. He will work with the nation's top financial leaders to jump-start the economy.

CHAPTER 20:
STUDY HALL

(Charlie and four other students from his history class have gathered to share notes and prepare for the midterm.)

Student #1: So, we know that the test will be 20 <u>multiple-choice</u> questions followed by an <u>essay question</u>.

Students #2: Right. And the essay question is 50 percent of the exam's grade. Now, do we have any idea what the essay's question topic will be?

Student #1: No, but we might be able to guess. Any ideas?

Charlie: I <u>wonder</u> if it will be on the <u>Roman Empire</u> and <u>Julius Caesar</u>. The professor really likes that topic.

Student #2: Maybe. I was thinking it's going be on <u>Alexander the Great</u>. The professor spent a lot of lectures on the details of his life.

Student #3: What if we all studied real hard on Alexander the Great, and then <u>Genghis Khan</u> <u>turned out</u> to be the essay topic?

Charlie: What if the question is on all three?

(The five students <u>hum</u> <u>simultaneously</u> in agreement.)

Student #1: That's gotta be it. The lectures focus a lot on the <u>empire</u> as a <u>reflection</u> of its leaders.

Student #4: I'm sorry to <u>interrupt</u>. Do you mean that the essay question will be on empires or the leaders?

Charlie: That's a good question. Hard to say.

Vocabulary

- <u>multiple choice</u> --- a question with a list of possible answers to choose from

- <u>essay question</u> --- a test question you answer with lots of writing

- <u>wonder</u> (think) --- to think and want to know more about sth.

- <u>Roman Empire</u> --- the area controlled by Rome from 27 BC - 476 AD

- <u>Julius Caesar</u> --- a famous Roman leader and general

- <u>Alexander the Great</u> --- a famous king and general of ancient Greece

- <u>Genghis Khan</u> --- a famous Mongolian leader and general

- <u>turn out</u> (happen) --- to happen in a special way

- <u>hum</u> (sound) --- to make a low sound for a period of time

- <u>simultaneously</u> --- at the same time

- <u>empire</u> (country) --- a group of countries controlled by one country

- <u>reflection</u> (sign) --- a sign of something

- <u>interrupt</u> --- to stop something for a short time

Comprehension Questions

1. What kind of test will the midterm be?
    - A. It will contain 20 questions, some of which are multiple-choice and some of which are essays.
    - B. It will contain 20 multiple-choice questions and one essay question.
    - C. It will contain 20 essays that you can choose to answer in multiple ways.
    - D. It will contain 20 questions.

2. Which three leaders were mentioned in the conversation in this chapter?
    - A. The Roman Empire, the Macedonian Empire, and the Mongol Empire
    - B. Charlie, Ben, and Lucy
    - C. Alexander the Great, Napoleon Bonaparte, and the professor
    - D. Julius Caesar, Alexander the Great, and Genghis Khan

3. Why is the essay question on the midterm so important?
    - A. Because there will be no final exam
    - B. Because it will count for half of the student's grade on the exam
    - C. Because the professor doesn't like multiple-choice questions
    - D. Because that's the only question on the exam

CHAPTER 21:
FROM A FOREIGN LAND

(The five students are currently on a break from reviewing. Charlie takes this opportunity to learn more about the foreign student in the group.)

Charlie: So, what's your name?

Lin: My name is Lin. Nice to meet you.

Charlie: Nice to meet you. Where are you from <u>originally</u>? ✓

Lin: I'm from China, but I came to the USA to study business and economics.

Charlie: Oh yeah? How's that coming along? ✓ 进展

Lin: Um, it's hard. I need to study more.

Charlie: Same here, but the more I study, the more <u>lost</u> I feel. It's hard for all of us.

Lin: Hmm, maybe some traveling could help. Have you ever traveled outside of your country?

Charlie: No.

Lin: I definitely recommend it. You learn so much about the world and yourself, too. It might help you find out what you really want.

Charlie: I like the <u>sound</u> of that.

Lin: You could always come to China!

Charlie: Learning Chinese sounds a little too hard. I was thinking about Europe, actually.

Vocabulary

- <u>originally</u> --- in the beginning

- <u>lost</u> (confused) --- not knowing what to do in a situation

- <u>sound</u> (idea) --- the idea that you get from something

Comprehension Questions

1. Why did Lin come to the USA?
    A. To study business and economics
    B. To start a business in the American economy
    C. To study international business and communication
    D. To start a business and economy consulting firm

2. Where has Charlie traveled to before?
    A. The Middle East
    B. Australia
    C. Antarctica
    D. None of the above

3. Traveling across the world can do all the following EXCEPT...
    A. teach you about yourself.
    B. teach you about the world.
    C. help you find out what the essay question is on the midterm.
    D. help you find out what you really want.

CHAPTER 22:
HOME SWEET HOME

(Charlie has just finished his <u>shift</u> at work and is getting ready to go home when he asks Lucy a question.)

Charlie: Hey, Lucy. Have you ever traveled abroad?

Lucy: Yeah, but it was a long time ago.

Charlie: Oh yeah? Where to?

Lucy: Sweden. I visited family there for a few months.

Charlie: Really? How was it?

Lucy: Very cold. <u>Good god</u>, it was cold! I had to wear a heavy coat while everyone else was wearing just <u>long-sleeved</u> shirts. It was crazy!

Charlie: Did you have fun while you were <u>freezing</u> at least?

Lucy: I loved it there. I went hiking all the time in the mountains. It was the most beautiful place I've ever seen.

Charlie: Wow. Why not live there longer, then?

Lucy: I grew up here in the US. I've learned that this is my home. It's where I belong.

Charlie: I'm not sure I feel the same. It's boring here. I've been thinking about doing some traveling myself, actually.

Lucy: Oh? Where to?

Charlie: No idea. Maybe Europe.

Lucy: You definitely should. It will give a whole new <u>perspective</u> on the world.

Charlie: Yeah. I wonder if I should do a study abroad program?
Lucy: I would. Do it before it's too late. Once you get married and have kids, it's game over! Forget about having a life at that point.

Vocabulary

- <u>home sweet home</u> --- used to say how happy you are to come home

- <u>shift</u> (time) --- a period of time you work

- <u>good god</u> --- *(informal)* used to show how surprised or angry you are

- <u>long-sleeved</u> --- having long arm coverings

- <u>freezing</u> --- very cold

- <u>perspective</u> (thinking) --- a way of thinking

Comprehension Questions

1. What does Lucy think about her time in Sweden?
    A. While it was extremely cold, she ultimately loved the trip.
    B. She hated everything about it.
    C. She was indifferent to the whole experience.
    D. While she got homesick occasionally, she had a wonderful time overall.

2. Why did Lucy move back to the United States?
    A. Sweden was too cold.
    B. It's where she feels she belongs.
    C. The taxes are too high in Sweden.
    D. The United States is a better country to start a family.

3. Living in a foreign country and attending a foreign university as a student is called...
    A. having a life.
    B. English abroad.
    C. study abroad.
    D. having a whole new perspective.

CHAPTER 23:

ICE CREAM BREAK

(While taking a break from video games, Charlie and Ben decide to go out for ice cream and take a walk through the park.)

Charlie: Wow, the weather is perfect today.

Ben: Yup, perfect for staying inside and gaming.

Charlie: I have a feeling you would say that no matter what the weather is.

Ben: But of course! Also, this ice cream is amazing. This strawberry flavor is so good!

Charlie: Strawberry's not bad. But I always end up choosing vanilla or chocolate. You can't go wrong with either.

Ben: Which did you get just now?

Charlie: I went with vanilla this time.

Ben: Ah. I wonder if they sell that ice cream in all three flavors.

Charlie: You mean chocolate, strawberry, and vanilla?

Ben: Yeah! I forgot the name of it. Uh, was it Napoleon flavor?

Charlie: Neapolitan.

Ben: Oh yeah. I thought it was Napoleon for a second.

Charlie: Now that would just be silly.

Ben: When you conquer half of the world at any given point in time, you tend to have a lot of things named after you, like the Napoleon complex.

Charlie: That is true. But wait. That makes me wonder. Why can't I think of anything named after Genghis Khan?

Vocabulary

- <u>have a feeling</u> --- to think or believe something

- <u>no matter what</u> --- used to say sth. is always true or sb. must do sth.

- <u>end up</u> --- to reach a place or situation after a long time

- <u>Napoleon</u> --- a famous French leader and general

- <u>silly</u> --- showing little to no thought

- <u>conquer</u> (control) --- to take control of foreign land by fighting

- <u>given</u> [preposition] --- already decided

- <u>tend</u> (be likely) --- to be true usually

- <u>name after</u> --- to give something the same name as something else

- <u>complex</u> (mental) --- a mental condition

Comprehension Questions

1. While on break from playing video games, what did Charlie and Ben do?
    A. They bought whipped cream and went jogging through the park.
    B. They bought shaving cream and took a walk through the amusement park.
    C. They bought ice cream and went for a stroll through the park.
    D. They took some time to study a little history.

2. Neapolitan ice cream contains which three flavors?
    A. cacao, blueberry, and vanilla
    B. chocolate, strawberry, and vanilla
    C. chocolate, strawberry, and villain
    D. cocoa, strawberry, and villain

3. According to Ben, when you conquer half of the world at any given point in time, ...
    A. you tend to have a lot of things named after you.
    B. you tend to have a lot of things naming before you.
    C. you tend to have a lot of things naming for you.
    D. you tend to have a lot of things named into you.

CHAPTER 24:
ESCAPING REALITY

(Charlie and Ben are chatting on the couch after finishing a gaming session.)

Ben: If you're going to go abroad, you have to go to Japan. It's a must. ✓

Charlie: I don't know. Japanese sounds pretty hard.

Ben: Bro, just get a Japanese girlfriend and you'll learn super-fast. You'll be completely immersed.

Charlie: If that were true, wouldn't all tourists come back fluent in Japanese?

Ben: A week or two isn't long enough. You'll be there for at least six months. Think about it. You get to enjoy all the latest games and anime the day they come out in Japan.

Charlie: Maybe. It's a possibility. But if all this sounds so good, why don't you go and study there?

Ben: The only thing I want to study is how to beat this boss we keep dying to.

Charlie: Don't you worry about your future?

Ben: That's future me's problem.

Charlie: You think of new ways to procrastinate every day, I swear. It's impressive, actually.

Ben: I'm just that good.

Charlie: What am I going to do with you?

Ben: Help me beat this boss, of course.

(Charlie <u>lets out a long sigh</u> and shakes his head slowly. After a few seconds of silence, he picks up his controller, ready to play again.)

Vocabulary

- <u>escape</u> (get away) --- to get away from something

- <u>reality</u> --- all real things

- <u>bro</u> --- *(informal)* a brother or a friendly way to talk to males

- <u>super</u> [adverb] --- very

- <u>immersed</u> (be involved) --- doing nothing but one thing only

- <u>tourists</u> --- people who visit a far away place for fun

- <u>fluent</u> (language) --- able to speak a language easily and well

- <u>procrastinate</u> --- to delay doing something you should do

- <u>swear</u> (promise) --- to promise you are telling the truth or will do sth.

- <u>impressive</u> --- makes you admire something

- <u>let out a sigh</u> --- to breath and relax after a difficult time

Comprehension Questions

1. Language immersion entails which of the following?
    A. Learning a language while immersed underwater
    B. Learning a language through non-stop exposure to the language
    C. Learning a language through immersive virtual reality
    D. Learning a language through tourism

2. Why does Ben think Charlie should travel to Japan?
    A. It's much better than China.
    B. He can enjoy all the latest anime and video games the day they are released in Japan.
    C. Japanese is the easiest language to learn.
    D. Japanese girlfriends are the best girlfriends to have.

3. How does Ben impress Charlie in this chapter?
    A. He is very persistent in persuading Charlie to go to Japan.
    B. He thinks of new ways to procrastinate.
    C. He thinks of a way they can beat the boss in the game.
    D. He is the strangest person Charlie has ever met.

CHAPTER 25:
CAR REPAIRS

(Charlie's car has been acting strange lately. He has brought it to a local mechanic to help diagnose and solve the problem.)

Mechanic: Hi there. What can I do for you today?

Charlie: Hello. My car has been acting up lately. When I stop at a traffic light, the whole car starts vibrating. As soon as I start moving, however, the vibrating stops. Other than that, the car has been running fine.

Mechanic: OK, I see. Let me take a quick look at it and give it a brief test run. In the meantime, have a seat over there in the lounge area. I'll come and get you when I'm ready.

Charlie: Alright. Thanks.

(While Charlie watches TV and makes himself a cup of coffee in the lounge area, the mechanic opens the hood of the car and takes a closer look at the problem. After around 30 minutes, the mechanic calls Charlie to the front desk.)

Mechanic: So, I checked the basics. I found that your oil is good. Your transmission is good. The tires are fine. The battery has no issues. There's no leakage anywhere. So, it's most likely a spark plug issue.

Charlie: Oh, that's good news! I thought it was the transmission.

Mechanic: Nope. Not at all. Now, we can replace all the spark plugs and ignition coils for you today with our special tune-up service. Would you be OK with that? ✓

Charlie: You need to replace the ignition coils too? How much will that cost?

Mechanic: Well, the tune-up service for this older model would keep your car running much longer. If we do the full tune-up, it will come to a total of $440.

Charlie: Oh my god! I'm not sure I can afford that. Can I make a phone call real quick?

Vocabulary

- mechanic --- a person who repairs machines

- diagnose --- to say what the cause of an illness or problem is

- act up --- *(people)* to behave badly, *(things)* to not work well 沮丧, 代性

- traffic light --- a set of red, yellow, and greens lights that control cars

- vibrate --- to shake softly and very quickly

- as soon as --- at the same time

- run (machine) --- to work well or cause a machine to work

- brief --- short

- test run --- a test to see how well something works

- in the meantime --- until or while something happens

- lounge --- a room for relaxing and waiting

- hood (vehicle) --- a cover for a vehicle's engine

- <u>call</u> (ask to come) --- to ask somebody to come somewhere

- <u>front desk</u> --- the desk inside of a building where guests or visitors go

- <u>transmission</u> --- the parts in a vehicle that pass the engine's power to the wheels

- <u>tires</u> --- the thick rubber ring part of wheels

- <u>battery</u> (device) --- a device that gives electrical power to machines

- <u>issues</u> (problems) --- problems with something

- <u>leakage</u> --- the escape of gas or liquid through a hole

- <u>spark plug</u> --- an engine part that lights gas and starts the engine

- <u>ignition coils</u> --- engine parts that give power to the spark plugs

- <u>tune-up</u> (engine) --- making small changes to an engine to improve it

- <u>model</u> (machine) --- a particular type of machine

- <u>come to something</u> (add up) --- to be the total amount after adding

Comprehension Questions

1. What is a synonym for the phrase "to act up"?

    A. To act strangely

    B. To act down

    C. To act accordingly

    D. To act fast

2. What appears to be the main problem with Charlie's car?

    A. The spark plugs have gone bad.

    B. The transmission is broken.

    C. The tires are flat.

    D. The ignition coils are not coiling.

3. Why does the mechanic recommend the special tune-up service?

    A. Because he wants to be Charlie's new friend.

    B. Because it could potentially help an older-model vehicle last longer.

    C. Because it will give the vehicle that new car smell.

    D. Because it will tune up the car so that it is ready for drag racing.

CHAPTER 26:
A SECOND OPINION

(Charlie is on the phone with his mom.)

Mom: Hello?

Charlie: Hi, Mom. I'm here at the car shop and was wondering if we have enough money to <u>cover</u> the repairs.

Mom: How much is it?

Charlie: Uh, $440.

Mom: <u>Oh lord</u>. What is the issue? What are they replacing?

Charlie: They said it's the spark plugs and maybe the ignition coils.

Mom: Honey, that does not cost $440 to fix. We could change all of that for less than $100.

Charlie: But they offered their tune-up service to make sure the car runs better.

Mom: That's called <u>taking advantage of</u> people. Mechanics know most people are not car-<u>savvy</u>, so they offer all kinds of expensive services to <u>drive up</u> the price. It's all <u>unnecessary</u> <u>crap</u> you don't need.

Charlie: Oh, OK. So, where should we get the car parts?

Mom: It's cheaper to order them online. Let's do that tonight.

Charlie: But how will I get to school tomorrow?

Mom: Well, I'll just have to drive you until the parts come in.

Charlie: That works. And, uh, I'm not sure what to tell Ben. He needs a ride to work tomorrow.

Mom: Ben got a job?

Vocabulary

- <u>second opinion</u> --- the opinion of a second expert to check the first

- <u>cover</u> (money) --- to be enough money for something

- <u>oh lord</u> --- *(informal)* used when you are surprised or worried

- <u>take advantage of somebody</u> --- to use somebody not in a fair way

- <u>savvy</u> [adjective] --- *(informal)* having knowledge of something

- <u>drive up</u> --- to make prices go up

- <u>unnecessary</u> --- not needed

- <u>crap</u> (junk) --- something that is worthless, useless, or bad quality

Comprehension Questions

1. What does Charlie's mom think about the mechanic's offer?
    A. She thinks Charlie should take advantage of the deal.
    B. She thinks another mechanic could offer a better deal.
    C. She thinks Charlie is taking advantage of the mechanic.
    D. <u>She thinks Charlie is being taken advantage of.</u>

2. If you are car-savvy, that means...
    A. you have little to no knowledge and experience with cars.
    B. you are knowledgeable and experienced with being gullible.
    C. you have a lot of knowledge and experience with cars.
    D. you are gullible when it comes to cars.

3. How will Charlie get to school tomorrow?
    A. Ben is going to drop him off.
    B. Ben is going to start working at a new job.
    C. His mom is going to drive him crazy.
    D. His mom is going to drop him off.

CHAPTER 27:

LEAVING THE NEST

(After fixing the car, Charlie and his mom relax by having some tea and eating some snacks.)

Charlie: That actually wasn't too bad. I thought it would be much harder than it was.

Mom: I told you so!

Charlie: Where did you learn all that stuff about cars? From Dad?

Mom: Absolutely not. I had to learn a lot on my own to survive as a single mom. You have to cut costs whenever you can.

Charlie: I figured that because he was good with electronic repairs he was also good with other kinds of machines.

Mom: He could have at least taught you some of that before he left.

Charlie: Yeah, well, he didn't. And that was a long time ago, right?

Mom: It's been about 10 years now.

Charlie: So, anywho, I think I've decided what I want to do college-wise.

Mom: Oh, what's that?

Charlie: I think I want to try studying abroad.

Mom: Oh. Where?

Charlie: I haven't decided yet, but I'm thinking somewhere in Europe.

Mom: What made you decide to travel?

Charlie: I feel like I have to go out on my own and start some sort of journey.

Mom: You could do that in this country, too. Just get a job and your own <u>place</u>.

(Charlie shuts his <u>lips</u> <u>tightly</u> and stares out the window as a long <u>pause</u> of silence fills the room.)

Mom: If you want to go, you'll have to find a way to pay for it. With your tuition fees, we're already <u>strapped for</u> cash <u>as-is</u>.
Charlie: Then I'll have to find a way.

Vocabulary

- <u>leave the nest</u> --- to move out of your parents' home

- <u>I told you so</u> --- *(informal)* used to say sb. should've listened to you

- <u>stuff</u> (skill) --- somebody's skills

- <u>on my own</u> --- alone

- <u>survive</u> --- to continue to live after a dangerous situation

- <u>figure</u> (think) --- to think

- <u>anywho</u> (anyway) --- *(informal)* anyway

- <u>place</u> (house) --- *(informal)* a house or home

- <u>lips</u> (body) --- the two soft edges of a mouth

- <u>tightly</u> --- closely or in a strongly controlled way

- <u>pause</u> (break) --- a short time where somebody stops doing sth.

- <u>strapped for</u> --- having little or none of something

• <u>as-is</u> --- as things are now

Comprehension Questions

1. Where did Charlie's mom learn about car repair?
    A. She learned from Charlie's dad.
    B. She taught herself in order to save money.
    C. She is a mechanic by profession.
    D. All single moms know how to fix a car.

2. Charlie's dad was skilled in what kind of repair?
    A. Electric
    B. Electrical
    C. Electronic
    D. Electricity

3. What made Charlie decide to travel?
    A. He wants to go find his dad.
    B. He wants to start a journey of sorts.
    C. He wants to find the love of his life.
    D. He wants to impress his mom.

CHAPTER 28:

THE BIG PROMOTION

(Charlie is at the pizza shop, <u>negotiating</u> a <u>promotion</u> to a <u>management</u> <u>position</u> with Lucy.)

Lucy: Are you sure about this? Don't do it unless you're 100 percent sure.

Charlie: I'm 100 percent sure. I have to <u>come up with</u> money <u>somehow</u>, and this will also allow you to take time off.

Lucy: I'm worried about whether or not you can <u>handle</u> the new level of stress that <u>comes with</u> being a manager. The <u>responsibility</u> of the job plus your schoolwork will <u>take a toll</u> on you over time.

Charlie: You said you'd promote me <u>in a heartbeat</u>, didn't you?

Lucy: I didn't think you'd actually want the job.

Charlie: Neither did I until recently. I feel like my life isn't going in any <u>direction</u> right now, so I need to fix that by saving money to travel abroad.

Lucy: You said that you'll leave a year from now to do that?

Charlie: That's right.

Lucy: Well, even if it's just a year, I'd rather have a <u>temporary</u> manager than no manager at all. So, <u>with that said</u>, <u>welcome aboard</u> Manager Charlie.

(Lucy <u>gladly</u> <u>extends</u> her hand and Charlie <u>confidently</u> puts out his to <u>meet</u> hers. They shake hands.)

Lucy: Let me <u>show you around</u> the office.
Charlie: <u>Sure thing</u>.

(<u>*Hidden*</u> *behind a* <u>*massive*</u> <u>*stack*</u> *of* <u>*paperwork,*</u> *Charlie notices a* <u>*framed*</u> *picture of a teenage boy, which is sitting on the desk.*)

Lucy: I think the best place to start is what you'll be doing the most as a manager here, which is <u>supervising</u> the staff. You tend to be pretty good at handling people, but let me tell you, this is a whole other level!

Vocabulary

- <u>negotiate</u> --- to talk business with sb. and try to agree on sth.

- <u>promotion</u> (job) --- giving sb. a more important job or position

- <u>management</u> (people) --- the people who control a business

- <u>position</u> (job) --- a job or level in an organization

- <u>come up with</u> --- to find an answer or the money to pay for sth.

- <u>somehow</u> --- for a reason or in a way that is not known

- <u>handle</u> (deal with) --- to deal with something

- <u>come with</u> (have) --- to have

- <u>responsibility</u> --- something that is your job to manage

- <u>take a toll</u> --- to hurt or make something weaker

- <u>in a heartbeat</u> --- very quickly and without thinking

- <u>direction</u> (development) --- the way something develops
- <u>temporary</u> --- lasting only for a short time
- <u>with that said</u> --- used to say what you've just said is less important
- <u>welcome aboard</u> (group) --- used to welcome a new member of a group
- <u>gladly</u> --- happily
- <u>extend</u> (stretch) --- to reach out or stretch something out
- <u>confidently</u> --- in a way that shows you believe in yourself
- <u>meet</u> (touch) --- to touch or join something
- <u>show somebody around</u> --- to guide somebody through a place
- <u>sure thing</u> (yes) --- used to agree with something
- <u>hidden</u> --- not easily seen or found
- <u>massive</u> --- very big, important, or successful
- <u>stack</u> (pile) --- things that have been put one on top of another
- <u>paperwork</u> --- written records and documents
- <u>framed</u> --- having a plastic, metal, or wood border
- <u>supervise</u> --- to manage people to make sure everything is done correctly

Comprehension Questions

1. When something takes a toll on you, it means that...
    A. it charges you a fee.
    B. it gives you money.
    C. it drains you of energy.
    D. it provides you with energy.

2. To do something in a heartbeat means...
    A. to do it while frightened.
    B. to do it immediately.
    C. to do it while panicking.
    D. to do it with passion.

3. What is on Lucy's desk in the office?
    A. Stacks of papers and a framed portrait
    B. Stacks of papers and a teenage boy
    C. Stacks of cash and Lucy's self-portrait
    D. Stacks of pizza boxes and burnt cheese

CHAPTER 29:
YOUR FREE CONSULTATION

(Charlie is at the counselor's office to find out more about the study-abroad program.)

Counselor: Have you ever traveled outside the country?

Charlie: I have not, ma'am.

Counselor: OK. And what do you expect to gain by <u>participating</u> in our program?

Charlie: I think studying abroad will help me find my <u>place</u> in the world.

Counselor: I think it absolutely can. Now, are you <u>willing</u> to study and learn a foreign language?

Charlie: Of course.

Counselor: Do you have any experience learning a new language?

Charlie: I took a few classes in high school.

Counselor: <u>Very well</u>. Do you have any questions for me about our program?

Charlie: I'm <u>curious</u>. How did you end up as a counselor here?

Counselor: Oh! Well, I went on my own study abroad trip to Ireland during college and loved every second of it. As a result, I wanted to help others have that same experience at least once in their lives.

Charlie: Ah, that's cool. Can I ask another question?

Counselor: Sure. What is it?

Charlie: Did you ever get <u>homesick</u> while abroad?

Counselor: Of course! But it's a small <u>price</u> to pay for a life-changing experience. There's a <u>saying</u> that <u>sums it up</u> quite <u>nicely</u>. In order to <u>truly</u> gain anything <u>meaningful</u>, something must be sacrificed.

Vocabulary

- <u>consultation</u> (meeting) --- a meeting to talk to an expert and get advice

- <u>participate</u> --- to take part in something

- <u>place</u> (role) --- a person's role in something

- <u>willing</u> --- ready to do something

- <u>very well</u> (agree) --- *(formal)* used to agree to something

- <u>curious</u> (interested) --- wanting to know something

- <u>homesick</u> --- sad because you are far away from home and miss it

- <u>price</u> --- the unpleasant things you must do or accept to get sth.

- <u>saying</u> --- a well-known phrase that gives advice

- <u>sum it up</u> --- to say the main points of something in short

- <u>nicely</u> (well) --- well

- <u>truly</u> (really) --- really

- <u>meaningful</u> (important) --- important, serious, or useful

Comprehension Questions

1. What does Charlie expect to gain by participating in the study abroad program?
    A. Help in finding his place in the world
    B. Help in finding the world
    C. Help in placing the world on himself
    D. Help in himself in his world placing

2. What kind of experience does Charlie have in learning a foreign language?
    A. He has no experience in learning a foreign language.
    B. He has a black belt in learning foreign languages.
    C. He took a few classes in high school.
    D. He took karate classes as a kid.

3. What does it mean to be homesick?
    A. To miss one's home while living abroad
    B. To be sick of one's home while living abroad
    C. To be sick while living at home
    D. To miss a day at work because one is sick

CHAPTER 30:

INTERVIEW WITH A POLYGLOT

(To learn more about language learning, Charlie has been watching videos on YouTube. One video in particular <u>catches his attention</u>. It's an interview with a <u>polyglot</u> who is discussing how he <u>came to</u> learn eight different languages.)

Interviewer: You're saying you didn't learn any of these languages through school?

Polyglot: That's correct. Spanish was the first one I learned. I took Spanish classes during <u>grade school</u>, but it felt like we were just <u>memorizing</u> lists of <u>vocabulary</u> words and grammar rules. Those classes did nothing to help me understand <u>spoken</u> Spanish or speak like a <u>native</u>.

Interviewer: So, how did you <u>go about</u> learning those things?

Polyglot: In college, I had a lot of free time <u>on my hands</u>. I got bored with watching TV and movies and playing video games after school, so I decided to do something more <u>challenging</u> with my time. I figured that <u>going all out</u> to learn Spanish would be the best thing I could do. I spent all my free time watching TV shows and movies in only Spanish, with no English <u>subtitles</u>.

Interviewer: Wow. How much of it could you understand at first?

Polyglot: <u>Practically</u> zero. It was very hard at first but also very exciting. After a few days of watching, I started noticing certain words and phrases were being repeated over and over. I wrote those down in my notebook and I <u>looked them up</u> online after each show ended. I kept repeating this <u>process</u> over and over. After a few months, I realized I could understand 90 percent of the Spanish in TV and movies. Shortly after, speaking <u>came very naturally</u>. I was so <u>amazed</u> by the learning process that I went out and <u>applied</u> the same <u>technique</u> to as many foreign languages as I could.

Vocabulary

- <u>catch somebody's attention</u> --- to interest someone

- <u>polyglot</u> --- a person who knows or uses many languages

- <u>come to something</u> --- to reach a particular situation

- <u>grade school</u> --- a school for kids from ages five to twelve

- <u>memorize</u> --- to learn sth. until you can remember it exactly

- <u>vocabulary</u> (language) --- all the words in a language

- <u>spoken</u> [adjective] --- said but not written

- <u>native</u> [noun] --- a person who was born in a particular area

- <u>go about something</u> --- to start or continue doing something

- <u>on my hands</u> --- having to manage something

- <u>challenging</u> --- difficult in a way that tests your abilities

- <u>go all out</u> --- to use all your energy to do something

- <u>subtitles</u> (language) --- words to explain what is being said in a film

- <u>practically</u> (almost) --- almost

- <u>look sth. up</u> --- to look for information using a book or computer

- <u>process</u> (actions) --- a list of steps you take for a particular purpose

- <u>come naturally</u> --- to be able to do something very easily

- <u>amazed</u> --- very surprised

- <u>apply</u> (use) --- to use something in a particular situation

- <u>technique</u> --- a particular way of doing something

Comprehension Questions

1. What was the polyglot's issue with Spanish classes?
    A. They were too expensive.
    B. They were too boring and dull.
    C. It felt like the teachers didn't care about what they were teaching.
    D. It felt like the students were just memorizing lists of words and grammar rules.

2. How did the polyglot learn Spanish during college?
    A. He spent all of his free time studying and getting the best grades possible in class.
    B. He spent all of his free time watching Spanish TV and movies with no English subtitles.
    C. He spent all of his free time watching English TV and movies with Spanish subtitles.
    D. He spent all of his free time memorizing lists of vocabulary words and grammar rules.

3. How did the polyglot learn the other foreign languages?
    A. He wrote down certain words and phrases over and over.
    B. He realized that he could understand 90 percent of any other language after learning Spanish.
    C. He repeated vocabulary and grammar rules over and over until he had memorized them.
    D. He applied the same technique to as many other foreign languages as he could.

ABOUT THE AUTHOR

Language Guru is a brand created by a hardcore language enthusiast with a passion for creating simple but great products. They work with a large team of native speakers from across the world to make sure each product is the absolute best quality it can be.

Each product and new edition represents the opportunity to surpass themselves and previous works. The key to achieving this has always been to work from the perspective of the learner.

DID YOU ENJOY THE READ?

Thank you so much for taking the time to read our book! We hope that you have enjoyed it and learned more about real English conversation in the process!

If you would like to support our work, please consider writing a customer review on Amazon. It would mean the world to us!

We read each and every single review posted, and we use all the feedback we receive to write even better books.

ANSWER KEY

Chapter 1:
1) B
2) D
3) C

Chapter 2:
1) A
2) B
3) C

Chapter 3:
1) D
2) D
3) C

Chapter 4:
1) B
2) A
3) D

Chapter 5:
1) C
2) D
3) C

Chapter 6:
1) A
2) D
3) D

Chapter 7:
1) D
2) A
3) D

Chapter 8:
1) B
2) A
3) B

Chapter 9:
1) C
2) A
3) D

Chapter 10:
1) B
2) B
3) C

Chapter 11:
1) C
2) A
3) C

Chapter 12:
1) A
2) B
3) B

Chapter 13:
1) D
2) B
3) D

Chapter 14:
1) C
2) C
3) C

Chapter 15:
1) A
2) C
3) A

Chapter 16:
1) D
2) A
3) B

Chapter 17:
1) B
2) A
3) B

Chapter 18:
1) D
2) D
3) D

Chapter 19:	Chapter 20:	Chapter 21:
1) C	1) B	1) A
2) B	2) D	2) D
3) A	3) B	3) C

Chapter 22:	Chapter 23:	Chapter 24:
1) A	1) C	1) B
2) B	2) B	2) B
3) C	3) A	3) B

Chapter 25:	Chapter 26:	Chapter 27:
1) A	1) D	1) B
2) A	2) C	2) C
3) B	3) D	3) B

Chapter 28:	Chapter 29:	Chapter 30:
1) C	1) A	1) D
2) B	2) C	2) B
3) A	3) A	3) D